In My Family

Faridah Yusof

In my family, my mom goes to work.

In Lan's family, her stepmom
works at home.

3

In my family, my brother walks me to school.

In Ben's family, his grandmother walks him to school.

5

In my family, my dad makes dinner.

In Jose's family,
his sister makes dinner.

In my family, my mom and dad and I read a story together.